Winning Ways

for Early Childhood Professionals

Understanding Infants

Gigi Schweikert

Name: ______________________________

Date: ______________________________

I0808304

Redleaf Press®
www.redleafpress.org
800-423-8309

Also in the Winning Ways series by Gigi Schweikert

Being a Professional
Partnering with Families
Becoming a Team Player
Understanding Toddlers and Twos
Understanding Preschoolers
Being a Supervisor
Supporting Positive Behavior
Responding to Behavior
Guiding Challenging Behavior

Published by Redleaf Press
10 Yorkton Court
St. Paul, MN 55117
www.redleafpress.org

First edition 2013
Cover design by Jim Handrigan
Cover photograph © Alloy Photography/Veer
Interior design by Erin Kirk New
Illustrations on page 48 by Becky Radtke
Photograph on page 4 by Amal Ayoub
All other photographs by Steve Wewerka
"A Child's Job" on page 21 and "A Message from the Book *Prime Times*" on page 67 are from *Prime Times* by Jim Greenman, Anne Stonehouse, and Gigi Schweikert (St. Paul, MN: Redleaf Press, 2008).
Printed in the United States of America

Library of Congress Cataloging-in-Publication Data
Schweikert, Gigi, 1962-
Winning ways for early childhood professionals. Understanding infants / Gigi Schweikert.
p. cm.
ISBN 978-1-60554-135-8 (alk. paper)
1. Education, Preschool—United States. 2. Child development—United States. 3. Child care—United States. I. Title. II. Title: Understanding infants.
LB1140.23.S35 2013
372.210973—dc23

2012032511

Printed on acid-free paper U17-11

Contents

From the Desk of Gigi Schweikert

That's me doing what I love most, working with children.

Dear Winning Ways Reader
(and Infant Teacher),

Recently my ten-year-old son asked me, "What's your favorite thing in the whole world besides me?" (I like the "besides me" part.) "That's easy," I quickly responded. "Babies. Babies are my favorite thing in the whole world, besides you, of course. I just love babies." So my son did a Google Images search for infants, and we spent the next hour marveling at the photographs. The way they look with their wide eyes of curiosity and awe of the world, babies seem to make everyone smile.

But working with infants is more than just thinking they're adorable. Being an infant teacher requires knowing and understanding infants, observing them closely, and responding appropriately to their subtle and not-so-subtle cues. An infant who is crying loudly is trying to tell you something. Being an infant educator is also an emotionally and physically demanding job. There's no nap-time in the infant room!

Whether you're new to the field or a veteran infant teacher, I think you'll like reading this Winning Ways book, *Understanding Infants*. You'll learn a few fascinating facts. I did while working on it. And you'll be reminded of how important your job as an early childhood professional really is. You provide infants with the care and nurturing they need to grow and flourish. You really do make a difference.

After you finish reading *Understanding Infants*, please send me your own thoughts, ideas, and stories about working with babies at www.gigischweikert.com. I'd love to hear them.

Children deserve our winning ways,

Introduction

What's the *Understanding Infants* Workbook All About?

Welcome to the Winning Ways book *Understanding Infants.* This book is one of three in the continuing series that includes *Understanding Infants, Understanding Toddlers and Twos,* and *Understanding Preschoolers.* You can read all three or work with the one that best helps equip you as an early childhood professional. This workbook is designed to help you

- Realize the amazing capabilities of infants
- Develop a better understanding of the development and growth of infants
- Improve your interactions with infants
- Create a more infant-appropriate routine and program

Who Are Infants?

For the purpose of this book, infants are considered children from birth to twelve months of age. Some professionals believe that infants become toddlers when they can walk. Some programs group infants according to age, and others adopt a multi-age grouping, especially common in family home care and education settings. In center programs, classroom rosters are often designated by many factors: ratios, size of rooms, availability of space in the next age group, and the developmental needs of the child. You may have children in your infant room who are eighteen months to two years old. Your role as the teacher is to help all children thrive, regardless of their classroom placement. If some infants in your care are becoming toddlers, grab another book in the series, *Understanding Toddlers and Twos,* to make sure you are creating an experience that is exciting and challenging to them.

Who Should Read and Use the *Understanding Infants* Workbook?

Understanding Infants is intended for anyone who works with infants or is thinking about working with them and anyone who works with adults who work with infants:

Veteran Educators Those of you who have worked with infants for many years and may even be caring for the children of the children they used to care for. That doesn't make you old, just seasoned!

New Teachers Those who have just started working with infants. As new educators, you are likely so excited about your role that most of you are eager to learn as much as you can and from as many sources as possible. This book is definitely for you!

Career Seekers Those who are considering becoming infant teachers. The early childhood field needs trained, enthusiastic, active individuals to care for and educate infants.

College Students Adult students in early childhood programs in colleges and universities.

Trainers Early childhood professionals facilitating seminars and workshops.

Professors Academics teaching adult students in early childhood programs in colleges and universities.

Program Supervisors Directors and other administrators who want to better support and train the staff in their infant programs.

winning ways

Using This Book

Understanding Infants is divided into eight topics that you can read in their entirety, or you can select a topic that helps with an issue for which you need guidance. Although reading the entire book will give you the greatest insight into understanding infants, each topic can stand alone as an educational or training tool. Here's what the book covers:

1. Working with Infants
2. Infants Are Amazing
3. Individualized Care for Infants
4. Interacting with Infants
5. How Infants Communicate
6. Helping Infants Settle and Sleep
7. How Infants Learn
8. Guiding Infant Behavior

Stressed-Out Teachers Those of you who need to be reenergized and educated about best practices for infants.

Parents Parents of infants who may not have experience raising children or the support of family nearby to help them.

Is the *Understanding Infants* Workbook Intended for Group or Individual Use?

Either way works great! You can use *Understanding Infants* as a training tool with a group or on your own. Either way, read through the appropriate content and complete the exercises throughout and at the end. Jotting down your answers will give you the greatest benefit from the workbook. If you are in a training group, having a written answer to refer to may help you feel more comfortable sharing your thoughts during the meeting.

DESIGN

How Is the *Understanding Infants* Workbook Designed for Training?

The workbook is designed so participants will

- Experience active learning by participating in discussions, solving problems, applying new knowledge to their current work situation, and getting reenergized about working in the early childhood field
- Connect current knowledge with the new material and have opportunities to talk about and share common concerns and issues regarding team building
- Gain practical knowledge and tips to begin using in their programs immediately

How to Use *Understanding Infants* in Trainings

You can use this book for a variety of training needs and situations. Here are some examples:

- Group of teachers from a classroom
- Administrative team
- Lunch and learn
- Staff meeting
- In-service day
- Partnership of several programs
- Community outreach
- Recruiting tool
- Local conference

SELF-ASSESSMENT

How Much Do You Understand about Infants?

Take a quick self-assessment to see how much you understand about infants. As a veteran early childhood professional, when I created the self-assessment, I was reminded and amazed about infant development, and surprised to learn through research a few things I didn't know. As you read each of the statements below and circle the frequency that best describes your understanding of infants, try to focus on how this information can help you improve your interactions with infants. Be honest with yourself. Just because you know something is good for infants doesn't mean you always do it. Understanding your current attitudes and actions toward infants is the starting point for improving your role as an infant teacher and making sure your interactions are positive and intentional.

1 I realize that my interactions with infants literally help to create the formation of their brains.

Always Usually Sometimes Never

2 I realize that infants are unique individuals who develop at their own pace and in their own way.

Always Usually Sometimes Never

3 I understand that infants need individualized care and education, not a routine in which all the infants do the same thing at the same time.

Always Usually Sometimes Never

4 My interactions with infants are positive, frequent, and deliberate.

Always Usually Sometimes Never

5 Although infants may not talk, I realize that their communication is complex and intentional.

Always Usually Sometimes Never

6 I realize that helping infants learn to move from awake to asleep and back again is an important part of the curriculum for infants.

Always Usually Sometimes Never

7 I help infants learn by offering them many opportunities to explore and responding to their interests and curiosities.

Always Usually Sometimes Never

8 I understand that discipline is not about punishment but about guiding infants to make safe choices and act in socially acceptable ways.

Always Usually Sometimes Never

Eight Steps to Understanding Infants

Refer back to your completed self-assessment form as you explore the eight topic areas for understanding infants. Whether you are on your own, reading and working at your leisure, or training with a group, you'll gain practical information you can use in the classroom and techniques for developing better interactions and relationships with infants. Let's get started.

1 Working with Infants

1

I realize that my interactions with infants literally help to create the formation of their brains.

- Always
- Usually
- Sometimes
- Never

Infant Teachers: Is That Term for Real?

Society, parents, and even early childhood professionals themselves often look at those who work with infants as babysitters, just caregivers, or pseudoteachers. Even in the early childhood field, infant teachers seem to get the lowest ranking on the imaginary education organizational hierarchy. Why? Maybe because caring for infants requires spending a great deal of time feeding, diapering, dressing, washing, and nurturing them. And without sounding too sarcastic, "How important could that be?" Well, I personally would like to thank all the adults in my infant life who helped me learn to eat, sleep, talk, and socialize, and who read to me, just to name a few tasks. Seems like some pretty important life skills to me! Guess you can sense my heart toward infant teachers.

Given that working with infants requires early childhood professionals to focus lots of time on what seems like "just caring" for infants, many professionals question, "Does that really make me a teacher?" You bet. The amount of learning that happens in the first year of life is exponential compared to any other time. You play an important role in helping infants interact with the world and the people around them, experience a sense of predictability, and develop a sense of trust and security through your consistent, positive actions. I'd say that makes you a professor of infants!

"You Do What?"

My Story about Being an Infant Teacher

I was an infant teacher many years ago. At a social gathering or family event, when someone asked me, "What do you do?" I initially responded proudly, "I'm an infant teacher." People were not only unimpressed and uninterested by my reply, but they often made comments like, "So you're kind of like a babysitter?" And then they would walk away to talk with someone whom they viewed as having a more meaningful and interesting job, like a lawyer or banker. Actually anything but what I did seemed more impressive.

One evening at a party at the New York Academy of Sciences—my husband is a scientist—I quickly tired of the fact that no one seemed to care about how I was changing the world one diaper at a time by working with infants. When the next person asked the usual question, "So what do you do?" I answered with, "I'm an NDS." Intrigued, the scientist asked me to tell him more. "Well," I explained with great pride, "I work hands-on with infants, interacting in a classroom-like setting, helping to enhance the development of neurons in the brain. It's quite complicated," I added. The questioner was impressed.

The next time I replied, "I'm an NDS" at one of those scientific functions, a man responded with, "Oh, wow, I've heard of that," which is impossible, since I made it up to impress people! Ha!

What Professions Does Our Society Value?

Think about it. What professions do you think that our society really values? Is infant teacher on the list? Here are some occupations that I thought of. See if you can add a couple more to the list. Do you notice that behind each of these titles is an abbreviation indicating the degree or title held by the profession or a word indicating the status of the occupation? In the cases following, the abbreviation usually refers to a degree, title, or special certification. Check them out and add a couple more you can think of.

- Doctor, MD
- Lawyer, Esq.
- Accountant, CPA
- Head of company, CEO

- Model, Super
- Sports figure, Nike
- ____________________
- ____________________

What's Behind Your Title?

Most early childhood professionals know and support the idea that well-trained teachers who continue learning throughout their careers provide better-quality education and care for infants. Although it is not necessary to have a degree or certification—I've seen some amazing teachers without them—even highly credentialed infant teachers can improve with further education. I suggest starting with the CDA, or Child Development Associate. With that said, what's behind your title? If I asked you to take out your business card, what would I find at the end of your name? I know—you're thinking, "I don't even have a business card." But if you did, what would be behind your name? Circle the best answer below.

BS   CDA   PhD   BA   ED   MA   Nothing

If you circled the word *Nothing*, that's not true. And even if you circled the majority of the degrees listed, I have an honorary degree for you all, an NDS. You are a neurodevelopmental specialist. Someone who helps develop the brains of infants. Really.

An NDS for You

You are . . .

- An NDS
- A Neurodevelopmental Specialist
- An Early Childhood Professional, NDS

The Role of a Neurodevelopmental Specialist, NDS

- Get those 100 billion brain cells moving.
- Have real conversations with children.
- Play with children.
- Read to children.

NDS

The Role of the Neurodevelopmental Specialist and the Infant Brain

Research The human brain is the most complex machine in the universe.

Implication If you are working with the most complex machine in the world, how can you not be important?

Research There are more cells in an infant's brain than there are stars in our Milky Way. That's about 100 billion brain cells.

Implication Your job is to get those brain cells moving by encouraging interactions with infants.

Research The infant's brain is not wired for learning at birth.

Implication If something is not complete, it has the potential to be complete. (Really look at the importance of the next two research points.)

Research The foundational networking of the brain's synapses is nearly complete after rapid brain development during the first three years of life.

Implication Since the brain develops the most during the first three years of life, your interactions with and responses to infants literally help to lay that foundation. Can you say, "NDS"?

Research The amount of connections in an infant's brain can increase or decrease by 25 percent depending on the environment and stimulation the child does or doesn't receive in the first three years.

Implication You can positively or negatively affect an infant by what you do and don't do.

Research An infant's first experiences imprint the child's genetic blueprint. That means that every interaction and experience from you or other adults has the capacity to help the brain develop to its fullest capacity.

Implication You need to know what you can do to make sure that happens. How will you interact? What will you say? How will you support the child? (The next two topics cover infant learning and positive interactions.)

Research An infant's early experiences are critical to the child's later intellectual and emotional potential.

Implication You help lay the foundation for what's to come!

Research The neural circuits that are consistently turned on over time will be strengthened.

Implication You help to strengthen those circuits with conversation, reading books, nurturing, and really everything you do. Cells that fire together wire together.

The Infant Brain

Every lullaby, every giggle and peekaboo triggers a crackling along an infant's neural pathways, laying the foundation for what could someday be a love of art or a talent for soccer or a gift for making and keeping friends. We know that babies who are hugged and feel loved and cared for are much more likely to grow up confident and optimistic. Each sound, sight, smell, taste, and touch physically alters the rapidly developing brain. And these changes forever influence how children perceive the world, the languages they will speak, and their capacity and ease for learning new information as adults. All that from working with infants? You bet. What's the best thing infants can experience for greater cognitive and physical growth? You should know the answer—you. The positive interactions with other people in children's early years play an important role in their development. An infant's best toy is you!

With Great Caution

Unfortunately, in situations where children are profoundly deprived of human contact and love, critical areas of the brain remain underdeveloped.

More on the Infant Brain: What Do Infants Really Know?

Although infants are born wired for vision, hearing, touch, smell, and taste, their experiences in infancy and throughout childhood complete the neuronal circuitry. What do infants really know? How can we, as educators, help them learn, grow, and, most importantly, develop a positive foundation for a lifetime of learning? Here's what you need to know about the senses:

Touch Touch is such a crucial sense that the area of the brain responsible for touch perceptions, the primary sensory cortex, can process tactile sensations by the fourth month of gestation. Skin nerves appear at week ten. At birth, the sense of touch is so developed that a baby will prefer soft flannel to rough textures.

Sight Although our society functions primarily based on the sense of sight, it's the slowest sense to develop. The world looks fuzzy to newborns, but by three months, a baby can follow moving objects.

Taste Taste buds appear at seven weeks' gestation. Taste preferences are shaped so early that even newborns have definite likes and dislikes. Infants have an acute sense of taste and generally prefer sweet. However, the specific tastes that the fetus is exposed to before birth through what the mother eats will shape a child's taste preferences.

Hearing Just as in taste, prenatal exposure to sounds penetrating the womb has a lasting effect on the infant's preference for sound. By twenty-eight weeks' gestation, the brain's auditory cortex, which receives input from nerve cells in the inner ear, can perceive loud noises. Newborns prefer their mothers' voice and can perceive every phoneme in the world's languages, an ability that is lost within the first year.

Smell Infants appear to develop a sense of smell even in the womb. Newborns will prefer a breast scented with amniotic fluid over one with only maternal scent, indicating they can probably smell amniotic fluid. Also, babies seem to locate their mother's nipples by smell. When they are presented with their mother's breasts, they are more likely to select the breast that smells like their mother over the other breast if it has been washed.

It's hard to grasp the immense amount of input and learning that is taking place for the infant in the first year of life. But it's not just learning; it's the formation of the framework for learning. Think about it like this. The hard drive of a computer sets the parameter of the computer's capabilities. The bigger the hard drive, the more the computer can do. The infant's brain is like the formation of an amazing hard drive. All that talk about computers and brains makes it sound like flashcards, worksheets, and teacher instruction will make all the difference for infants. Actually, that's not the case at all. Infants need positive, predictable, nurturing interactions in a language-filled setting. Next, I describe positive ways that you can better help infants during this critical time.

OPTIMIZE YOUR KNOWLEDGE

1 Explain why you believe people **do not always value** the work of those caring for infants.

____

____

____

____

2 List three specific reasons why you play a role in the **continuing formation** of the infant brain.

1 ______________________________

2 ______________________________

3 ______________________________

3 Describe the **most interesting fact** you learned about babies from reading this chapter and how knowing that information influences your work with infants.

____

____

____

____

2 Infants Are Amazing

2

I realize that infants are unique individuals who develop at their own pace and in their own way.

- Always
- Usually
- Sometimes
- Never

Every Baby Is Different

Although infants have distinct, sequential developmental characteristics, each infant is special. A mom of identical multiples will tell you that. So as you discover more about how infants develop, keep in mind that there is a wide variation in individual differences. Each baby has unique qualities, and your response to and interaction with each infant will be as varied as the infants themselves.

4 Things Every Infant Learns to Do

1 Make sense of the world From what researchers understand, the world to a newborn baby is not clearly defined through sight, sound, touch, smell, and taste. Instead, it is a blooming, buzzing confusion, with everything blending together and flowing into the nervous system as waves of sensation. The task of separating and sorting sensations begins at birth and continues as infants refine their senses and learn to make finer distinctions. They learn to communicate quickly in many different ways. They try to engage you with their smiles and cries. Who can resist a baby? They attempt to grab your attention, and even the most serious of people usually become cooing personalities when confronted with an infant. Infants are experimenting with many strategies to communicate with the world and receive their desired outcomes.

Did You Know? Fascinating Facts about Infants

Babies are born with 300 bones, but we adults only have 206 bones in our bodies. What happens to the other 94 bones? Many bones are not fully developed at birth and fuse together as they grow, like the skull.

How would you like to double your weight in six months? I could probably do that if I went on a few vacations. Newborns double their birth weight in half a year. And by the end of their first year, most infants have tripled in weight. Babies also have heads that account for about 25 percent of their total weight; 25 percent of my total weight is not in my head.

Would you say that most infants usually prefer fruits or vegetables when they begin solid food? If you said fruit, you are correct. Babies seem to have an innate preference for sweetness. As early as thirteen weeks after conception, an embryo can detect taste differences. The gulp rate of amniotic fluid increases in the presence of sweetness.

Are you a righty or lefty? Around ten weeks of age, a baby develops a tendency toward being right- or left-handed.

Babies always seem to have really big eyes. They do. Infants are born with eyes the approximate size of their adult eyes. Although the size of eyes may not grow much, their noses and ears grow their entire lives. Guess that's why you never see a baby with a large nose.

Ever notice that when newborns cry, there are no tears? That's because the body doesn't begin to produce tears in response to emotion until the infant is between eight and sixteen weeks.

2 **Understand how things work** Curiosity is a powerful human trait, and young children are born with a drive to discover. They respond to the world with a scientific approach of trial and error, constantly assessing: "If I do this, then what happens?" Babies poke, suck, and drop things—this is learning.

3 **Discover and develop their physical attributes** Babies are learning about their bodies and how they work. Their hands and feet fascinate them. Infants learn to hold their heads up, discover their hands, develop their grasp, and eventually creep around the room.

4 **Connect with others** Babies need to connect with other people. Because infants are completely dependent on others for their care and protection, they must connect with other people. Infants try to bond through their sounds, gestures, smiles, and murmurs. Most adults respond with appreciation and a concern for their well-being.

How Important Are Developmental Milestones?

A Personal Developmental Milestone Assessment

For the following questions, please indicate the chronological age at which you first achieved these developmental milestones:

1. How old were you when you could lift your head up with assistance? ____
2. At what age could you roll over? ____
3. When did you learn to sit up? ____
4. When did you learn to pull up to a standing position? ____
5. At what age were you toilet trained? ____

The Journey Starts Here

Are you thinking that you have no idea when you reached these milestones in your life? Some of you may know when you achieved these steps, and most of you will not. Does it really matter? When did you take your first step? Were you a biter, or maybe the victim of a biter? When did you start using words? And just for the record, when were you toilet trained?

During the early years and especially the first year, you watch development closely, caring intensely about many things, as an early childhood professional should. However, many of these things have no developmental importance. There is no future developmental advantage and rarely any significance to early achievement of most milestones. Typical development assumes many different forms and proceeds at a pace appropriate to each child. Yes, you should look for signs of possible developmental delays that signify physiological problems, but take care that alertness does not create a climate of comparison, competition, and worry. Appreciate all children for who they are, celebrating their accomplishments without always anticipating mastery of emerging skills. Enjoy the now.

- Recognize and delight in the mastered and emerging skills of infants.
- Provide many opportunities for children to practice and perform these skills.
- Help when children are frustrated or approaching frustration.
- Enjoy their success and achievements.

"A Child's Job"

A Note from Jim Greenman*

A child's job is to learn all about the world and fully develop into the very best person that he or she can be.

Think about children as being born with a job to do. *Their job is to learn about the world and develop into the very best people that they can be.* Children are fully equipped and driven to pursue that job. They are filled with possibilities. From birth, they are marvelous learners, immediately investigating the sights, sounds, and feel of the world. They are born to be competent little scientists, driven to move, to experiment, to know. They also are programmed to connect with and learn from the people around them . . . Children are in a state of constant learning long before an infant's first steps and first words; long before toddler's first real social play and first sentences; long before the plunges into reading, writing, sports, and a complicated social life that mark children's development in preschool and early school-age years—long before they are given the label *students*. As they move through childhood, they are exploring all their own bodily powers and what the world is made of: sensations, people, things, relationships, and the elements and forces of the natural world.

* Jim Greenman was one of my favorite early childhood professionals. He encouraged me to start writing, and we coauthored *Prime Times* together.

The Many Things Infants Can do

Here are some small- and large-motor skills you will usually see infants exhibit in this sequential order.

Motor-Skill Development

Small-Motor	Large-Motor
Discover hands and feet	Lift head
Mouth hands and fingers	Roll over
Grasp an adult's finger	Push up on arms
Transfer toys from one hand to the other	Sit up
Pick up small food pieces	Crawl
Feel textures such as bumpy material, sandpaper, or smooth plastic	Pull up
String beads	Stand
Scribble on paper	Cruise, holding onto objects
	Walk (Most children walk at twelve months, but range is nine to sixteen months.)

50 Things Infants Can Do

1 Babble
2 Bang
3 Bend
4 Clap
5 Coo
6 Crawl to, in, out, over
7 Creep around, in, under
8 Cry
9 Drop things
10 Eat
11 Experiment
12 Feel
13 Find
14 Follow an object with their eyes
15 Grasp
16 Hear
17 Hold
18 Imitate sounds and simple actions
19 Inspect
20 Kick
21 Knock away
22 Lift head up
23 Listen
24 Look
25 Look for
26 Mouth
27 Pinch
28 Pull up
29 Put in
30 Reach for
31 Reach out
32 React to others
33 Recognize people and things
34 Rock
35 Roll
36 See
37 Shake
38 Sit up
39 Sleep
40 Smell
41 Solicit from others
42 Squeeze
43 Swing
44 Take out objects
45 Taste
46 Tear
47 Touch
48 Transfer from one hand to the other
49 Turn
50 Watch

What else can you add to the list? You only have to observe infants for a few minutes to observe the many things they can do.

Assessing the Infant's Experience

It's not enough to understand infant development. Your responsibility is to take that information and construct a program that focuses on developmentally appropriate experiences for the children—not what's most convenient for you or the structure of the planned routine. Take a look at the statements below and determine how your program rates.

The Infant's Experience

1 The program adjusts to each infant's schedule instead of all the children being on the same schedule. For example, infants sleep when they are sleepy and eat when they are hungry.

Our strength Our work-in-progress Our goal

2 The infants go outside every day in all kinds of weather, even in light rain and snow. Parents' preferences, along with licensing requirements and geographical norms, are taken into consideration.

Our strength Our work-in-progress Our goal

3 The time that infants spend in bouncy seats, swings, and high chairs is limited, and infants are frequently placed on their tummies to play each day.

Our strength Our work-in-progress Our goal

4 Teachers make interacting one-on-one with infants and in small groups a priority. Time is set aside each day to hold and cuddle babies, even when they are not in distress.

Our strength Our work-in-progress Our goal

5 Opportunities for exploration and learning are built into the environment.

Our strength Our work-in-progress Our goal

6 Teachers read to infants many times a day.

Our strength Our work-in-progress Our goal

What Type of Experiences Are Infants Having in Your Program?

For the area(s) that you answered, "Our strength," keep up the good work! Feel good that the infants in your care are getting a great experience in that area. For the statements in which you rated your program "Our work-in-progress," list three ways that you can improve the situation and start making it happen. For example, if *Teachers read to infants many times a day* is your "work-in-progress," you can make it your "strength" by placing books to read to infants throughout the room, having certain times of day that you read, maybe after every meal, and by keeping a chart of the infants and marking that you read to each one at least three times a day. Make sense? If "Our goal" was your answer, it's time to make some changes in this area. Set a date by which you will make sure it happens.

Do You Expect Babies to Act Like Babies?

Creating a good place for infants—one that is a relaxed, nurturing, and learning environment—depends on having appropriate expectations. This means expecting infants to behave like infants. Expect babies to

Be different from each other Children will differ in interests, moods, pace, ability to signal how they feel, how they learn, how they react to change, and the care they need.

Cry to communicate Crying is the way infants let us know they need our help. They don't cry just to annoy us.

Desperately need you Being allowed to remain in distress is not good for infants and is likely to lead to increased crying. It works against the feeling of basic trust and security that provide the foundation for healthy development.

Explore A continuous curiosity fuels the process of learning about the world.

Test all limits Babies learn how the world works by testing the reactions of people and things to their actions.

Experiment with their bodies They use their growing physical powers to test the properties of people, things, and space. They need to crawl, walk, run, kick, step up and down, move, stack, drop and throw things, take things apart, fit themselves and things inside other things, and climb in and over, if they are to learn.

Experiment with their senses The mouth, eyes, ears, and skin are the tools babies use to learn. They need to touch, taste, feel, look, and listen to the world. Babies' mouths and whole bodies are their chief tools, such as sucking on most things and testing the feel of things on their cheeks and even stomachs. Ever see infants smear baby food on their tummies? Why? So they can better understand how baby food feels.

With Special Care

Steps for Identifying a Child with Special Needs

Since the typical range of development is quite wide for infants, many special needs are not evident to the parents or even the child's pediatrician until children enter group care. If you have a concern that an infant in your care may have a condition beyond what is typical and that he may benefit from early recognition and intervention, complete the following steps:

1. What behavior does the child exhibit that concerns you? Or is it the absence of a behavior that concerns you?

2 Document the occurrence. Describe the behavior. Indicate the situation in which it happens. Note the date and time. Or describe the behavior that the child is not exhibiting.
3 Compare the child's behavior or absence of behavior to developmental norms.
4 Bring your concern to the attention of your supervisor.
5 Respect the child and his family by maintaining confidentiality and limiting conversations with colleagues unless it concerns them.
6 With the support of your supervisor, bring your concerns to the parents, recognizing the potential for emotional response, denial, or even deflecting the issue back on you or the program.
7 Develop a plan for more observation.
8 Request permission from the parents to consult outside resources.
9 Learn how to better assist the child in your environment.
10 Celebrate the abilities of the child.

Every Infant Is Special

Of course, all infants are special and have special needs, but some children have conditions that require attention beyond that of the typically developing child. You may have infants in your program who have

- Developmental delays, like motor delays
- Disabling conditions
- Chronic illnesses or medical conditions
- Family situations that put them at some risk

A good early childhood program is never "one size fits all," but rather one in which you meet the needs of children with individual consideration and program adaptation.

- Observe and get to know the child.
- Respond to the cues of the infant.
- Focus on and build off the strengths of the infant.
- Take your time when interacting with the child.
- Be flexible and innovative.

Read back over the list above. Aren't those things that you should do as you work with every infant? That's the definition of individualized, good-quality education and care.

12 Guidelines for Caring for Infants with Special Needs

1 Your responsibility is to provide good-quality education and care based on infants' individual needs, as with all children.

2 Recognize and understand your own feelings. You may feel sadness and pity or even anger or disgust.

3 Grow to accept the infants and have a more relaxed attitude toward their education and care.

4 Learn about the special need.

5 Ask the parents about caring for their children. Write the questions down if that helps you feel more prepared.

6 Offer to speak with other professionals the family uses to learn more about caring for their children.

7 Respect the parents' right to share or not share information with you.

8 Let the parents know that you are committed to helping their children have a positive experience in the program.

9 Reassure and support the parents' feelings and needs.

10 Adapt your program to fit the infants so that they can participate and be challenged without being overprotected or separated from the group.

11 Develop an individual care plan that helps them reach their fullest potential.

12 Let others help you care for the infants. Often when teachers feel comfortable caring for them, they tend to develop a strong emotional attachment. It is important that the children develop relationships with other adults and children in the program too.

winning ways

Infants have amazing capabilities and grow and learn at rates that are almost unfathomable to adults. Ever feel a bit frustrated when an older infant is constantly knocking things off the shelf, only to remember that the child has only been on this earth for less than a year? Ever get so busy that you forget that holding infants, even if they are not crying, is good for them? Your positive interactions help infants develop the self-esteem and skills that fit their unique personalities, provide the children with the foundation for social competence and well-being, and give you a deep personal satisfaction. The next topic is individualized care and education for infants.

OPTIMIZE YOUR KNOWLEDGE

1 Write a **job description** for infants. Include at least five job responsibilities infants have.

____

____

____

____

____

2 Large-motor development is typically sequential, meaning it happens in a certain order. Put the following **large-motor skills** in order of when most infants achieve them:

___ Crawls

___ Sits up

___ Walks

___ Lifts head

3 Imagine that you have a three-month-old infant who is still having difficulty supporting his head without assistance. Describe **what you would do** to further assess the situation and help the infant and family if necessary.

____

____

____

____

3 Individualized Care for Infants

3

I understand that infants need individualized care and education, not a routine in which all the infants do the same thing at the same time.

- Always
- Usually
- Sometimes
- Never

One Size Does Not Fit All: The Importance of Individualized Care

Although individualized care and education are important for all children in early childhood education, they are particularly significant for infant care. A group of infants does not and should not have a daily routine that everyone follows. Toddlers and older children tend to eat around the same time, have an afternoon nap, and head outside as a group. Good infant care requires that all infants have their own schedule and that the infant teacher responds individually to each child. At any given time in an infant room, one infant may be sleeping, another playing on the floor, and another having a bottle.

It would be easy for teachers to merely move from crying infant to crying infant, responding to their needs for food, sleep, or changing. Responding to infants' needs is important, but *anticipating* and then responding is even better. Infants should receive your care and attention not just as responses to their crying but as a deliberate internal desire to be with and interact with them.

Giving Infants Individualized Care

But with so many babies and teachers—six infants and two teachers or eight infants and two teachers, in the best circumstances—how do all infants get the care and education they desire and need? Human interactions are the core of any good infant program, and you need systems to ensure that each infant experiences those human interactions from you and the other teachers. I believe that the primary caregiving system is the most helpful and effective way to ensure individualized care, and I'll discuss that at length, but there are other ways to ensure continuity of care. Take a look at the following ideas.

9 Ideas for Ensuring Continuity of Care and Education

The main goal of excellent care is to ensure that all infants sense and receive consistent, predictable care based on their individual needs and communication signals. This goal is especially important in programs with high staff turnover, inconsistent staffing schedules, or frequent movement of children into or out of the program. Programs can provide children with consistency of care and security through the following:

1. **Establish a primary care system.** Pair an infant with one particular teacher who develops an ongoing relationship with the child and the family. This is something that typically happens by default in family child care settings.
2. **Have familiar teachers scheduled during drop-off.** If programs are unable to provide one primary caregiver, establish a schedule so that babies see the same familiar faces in the morning.
3. **Develop a separation ritual.** Separation can set the tone for the day. A consistent ritual that is established for transitioning children from parents to program will make separation easier for children and adults.
4. **Establish a bond between family and program, not just a particular room.** Children should connect with the teachers in their room, as well as with other members of the staff. By seeing familiar smiles of administrators or administrative assistants in the lobby or foyer, children and their parents will come to feel like they belong to the whole program. The relationship is helpful when children move to new rooms, administrative staff step in to cover ratios, or problems arise that require the help of the director or other support staff.
5. **Keep ratios and group sizes small.** It is easier for infant teachers to observe and respond to infants' needs if there are fewer children to care for.
6. **Have children remain with the same teachers as they age.** Whenever possible, have children stay with the same group of teachers and change the room, experiences, and challenges to meet the needs of the children, not the teachers' convenience or preconceptions of "this has always been an infant room."

7. **Consider mixed-age grouping as a means for meeting consistency.** Children will stay in the same room and with the same teachers for a longer period of time. Although teachers and parents are often reluctant to participate in mixed groups, believing that the older group has more to offer, family child care providers and good programs make multiage groups work.
8. **Develop a staff organizational structure that positions a supervisor in each room.** In programs that have high turnover, it may make sense to identify a more experienced infant teacher who can be given greater responsibility. People who strive for and are capable of supervisory roles are usually dedicated to the early childhood career and are more likely to stay with the program.
9. **Create systems for sharing children's care preferences.** A primary caregiver learns to read the sleep, eating, diapering, and other care routine cues and preferences of the children in her care. Create, post, and continually update care information about each child for all teachers to use. Ask for parents' input as well. For example, note that one likes to be helped to sleep with a teddy bear and a back rub. Remember that some information may be confidential or sensitive, so position that information where only teachers have access and not other parents or visitors.

What Is the Primary Caregiving System?

In the primary caregiving system, each child has an assigned primary teacher who develops a special relationship of mutual trust and respect with that child and the infant's family. As the primary caregiver, you become an expert, advocate, and coordinator of the child's and parent's experience. But work with other teachers to ensure a positive education experience. The goal is that all infants get the attention they deserve and that no child is unintentionally ignored or receives less attention and care.

Let's Be Honest

I know through my own teaching experience, and you have probably felt this, too, that you are drawn to certain children and families and easily establish relationships with them. Other children and families are hard to get to know. Primary caregiving systems help your program connect to every child, even those who may be harder to love because of their constant demand for attention, their appearance, or even their smell. Sounds harsh? No. It's the reality of human nature and relationships, and that's why systems that ensure individualized, consistent care are so important.

A Word of Caution

"Primary" Does Not Mean Exclusive

You don't want infants to become totally dependent on the presence of one person in order to have a good day. Primary caregiving is not the same as a small-group structure, and children do not spend the day at their primary caregiver's side, like chicks next to a mother hen. Other teachers develop a warm relationship with the infants and have caring and learning interactions with them as well.

"Primary Caregiver" Does Not Mean "Primary Teacher"

The primary caregiver is not the only influence over the child. The primary care system is just one system that promotes good-quality care and education. A primary caregiver does not determine the child's learning experience. The educational experience of all the infants, the caregiving practices and systems, and the other elements of good-quality care are planned and developed by the leadership staff, who have the training and experience in program planning. Primary caregiver is a role that staff at all teaching levels can have.

The 5 Key Roles of a Primary Caregiver

The key roles of the primary caregiver are outlined below. Think about the ones you are currently playing in the life of each infant, and explore the ones you may need to develop or enhance.

1. **Communicate.** Share information about infants with their family and appropriate staff.

   You are the essential link in the communication chain between families and program and infants and program. You ensure that each day, the infants' experience is communicated to the parents—not just what you witnessed, but what others observed or enacted. You relay parents' concerns and suggestions to other teachers.

2. **Advocate.** Speak for the infants and their parents.

   You empower parents and children by translating their individual concerns and needs into action through the efforts of all program staff. You ensure that the program "wraps around" infants and their families rather than insisting that they fit the program.

3. **Nurture.** Love and care for infants.

   You tune in to infants and develop a special bond that ensures all needs are met. You ensure that these are carried out in ways that empower infants and establish a sense of security and basic trust.

4 Facilitate learning. Help infants learn.
You care for each infant in a manner that maximizes language experiences and the learning potential of all interactions. You ensure that the learning environment works for that child with a balance of developmentally appropriate experiences that are not overly or insufficiently stimulating.

5 Observe, monitor, and evaluate. Ensure that the infants and families have a positive experience.
You make sure that infants' experience in the program is positive and that the concerns of families are addressed by continually assessing the child-and-family experience. You monitor the care and education infants actually receive rather than their presumed experience.

Basic Knowledge for Primary Caregivers

Although your program may not currently have a primary caregiving system, look at the assessment below and see if you have the basic knowledge you need to be a primary caregiver. If you do this assessment with your classroom team, you might find that certain teachers know more about certain children and that you can establish an informal primary caregiving system.

10 Things Primaries Should Know about Children and Families

Primary caregiver's name: ______________ Date: ____________

Program: ________________________ Room: __________

1 I know the full names and ages of all the infants in my primary care. ☐ yes ☐ no

Names and ages I need to learn:

____

____

2 I know the daily schedule of all the children in my primary care. ☐ yes ☐ no

Daily schedules I need to learn:

____

____

3 I know the developmental skills, abilities, and special needs of all the infants in my primary care. ☐ yes ☐ no

Developmental skills, abilities, and special needs I need to learn:

____

____

4 I know the individual personality traits, moods, and interests of all the infants in my primary care. ☐ yes ☐ no

Individual personality traits, moods, and interests I need to learn:

____

____

5 I know the family and child food preferences and food sensitivities of all the children in my class. ☐ yes ☐ no

List the name of all infants and any food sensitivities or allergies they may have.

____

____

6 I know the diapering and toileting needs of all the infants in my primary care. ☐ yes ☐ no

List the name of each infant and any parent preferences concerning diapering and toileting needs.

____

____

7 I know the sleeping needs of all the infants in my primary care. ☐ yes ☐ no

List the name of each infant and any child or parent sleeping preferences.

____

____

8 I know the preferred play and learning experiences of all the infants in my primary care. ☐ yes ☐ no

Preferred play and learning experiences I need to learn:

____

____

9 I know the guidance and socialization patterns or effective teaching methods for all of the infants in my primary care. ☐ yes ☐ no

Guidance and socialization patterns I need to learn:

____

____

10 For each family, I know names and schedules, values and priorities for their child, concerns and sensitive issues, and daily information they want to know about their infant. ☐ yes ☐ no

Names of parents and schedules that I need to learn:

____

____

Names of parents and specific concerns and issues:

____

____

Daily information each parent desires:

____

____

How did you do? You may actually know this information about all the infants in your care, especially if you work in family child care or have a small group of six babies. The system is not as important as knowing each child.

How to Make the Primary Caregiving System More Successful

Assign primary caregivers according to the following:

- Compatibility of parents' and teacher's schedules. *Will they see each other?*
- Roughly balanced number of children of varying ages for each caregiver. *Do the teachers have somewhat equal groups of children?*
- Likely demands of children upon the teacher. *If a child has special needs, are these taken into consideration?*
- Compatibility of parent, staff, or child characteristics. *Is this a good match between parent and teacher and infant and teacher?*

And keep in mind:

- An alternative primary caregiver should be designated for children when the teacher is absent. *Is there someone else to write a daily experience sheet and have conversations with the family?*
- Avoid creating relationships that are so close that infants have a horrible day when the teacher is not present. *Are the infants attached to and comfortable with other teachers?*

Individualized care and education are very important for infants and early childhood professionals! They ensure that all children get the attention they need and deserve. Try using a primary caregiving system if you don't have one in your program, and at the very least, have systems in place that ensure continuity of care and that give all infants advocates. Now that you understand the importance of individualized care for each infant, let's talk about interacting with infants.

OPTIMIZE YOUR KNOWLEDGE

1 Why is **continuity of care** important?

____

____

____

____

2 Why do some infants get **more attention** than others? Do not list the names of children or their families, but create an honest list.

____

____

____

____

3 How can you ensure that each infant in your care has an **advocate**? Develop a system and explain how it works.

____

____

____

____

4 Interacting with Infants

4

My interactions with infants are positive, frequent, and deliberate.

- Always
- Usually
- Sometimes
- Never

Interactions: Positive and Frequent

In good-quality early childhood programs, an almost constant interaction exists between infants and teachers. As you're changing their diapers, you are caring for them, talking to them, and reassuring them. You do all that, but many may see only the necessary task of diapering, not one of great educational importance for the child. Yet interactions and learning are inseparable. Education is a result of responsive, language-filled interactions during care routines and anytime, really, coupled with an appropriate learning environment. For infants, this means an environment full of materials for exploration and developmentally appropriate challenges.

Learning All the Time

Infants are learning all the time, including during care routines and transitions. Since they can learn from everything, take your time to observe them. Respond to their interests and explorations, play with them, support them, and enjoy working with them. When teachers of infants are having fun and delighting in reciprocal interactions, children are connecting to others. Could there be greater learning than that?

Interacting with Infants: Six Opportunities That Make a Difference

Obviously, anytime is a good time for you to interact with infants, except, of course, if they are sleeping—everyone knows "never wake a sleeping baby." In group education and care, you must be intentional about seeking opportunities to connect with individual infants in a meaningful and purposeful way. There are certain times when you can be more engaged and can really focus on them. Use the following "captive moments" to make sure you are interacting with each infant:

Separation: redirecting and calming the infant, and explaining what is happening

Care times: feeding, changing a diaper, dressing, and soothing to sleep

Quiet times: reading books, singing lullabies, looking out the window

"Ah-ha" times: encouraging moments of exploration and discovery

Floor time: describing play, asking questions

"You are special" times: telling the infant about himself, appreciating and celebrating his uniqueness

Positive Interactions with Infants

10 Essential Times

Both infants and teachers initiate interactions. Even very young infants initiate social interactions through crying, looking, visually following, and later through vocalizing and gesturing. From birth, babies also respond to social approaches from adults. Crying infants often stop crying when you pick them up. Infants settle and become still as they listen to you talk or sing. They respond with smiles and coo contentedly when you soothe them with smiles and cuddles.

Responsiveness to infants' initiatives is critical, so how do you respond?

Assess Yourself

1 I take my time when I am working one-on-one with an infant, whether diapering, feeding, or interacting in other ways.

Always Usually Sometimes Never

2 I talk directly to infants, not over their heads to other adults. *I'm going to change your diaper now so you'll feel more comfortable, instead of I'll change these three if you change those two.*

Always Usually Sometimes Never

3 I tell infants what I am going to do as I am caring for them. *I'm going to wash your hands. Does the water feel a little cool? Let's use this paper towel to dry them now.*

Always Usually Sometimes Never

4 I offer infants the opportunity to help as much as they can. *You can help me. You hold the clean diaper until I am ready to put it on you.*

Always Usually Sometimes Never

5 I acknowledge my own tolerance for noise, crying, smells, and even physical appearances.

Always Usually Sometimes Never

6 I speak positively to children about unpleasant care routines, such as dirty diapers or food that I don't like the smell of. I avoid saying things like *What a stinky diaper you have* and *I don't know what kind of baby food this is.*

Always Usually Sometimes Never

7 I am willing to compromise my own personal feelings about care to adapt to infants' needs and parents' preferences. I avoid judgments like *This baby is held too much* or *I don't understand why your mother wants you so dressed up all the time.*

Always Usually Sometimes Never

8 I pay attention to my body language and avoid rude behavior, knowing that body language can be more powerful than words. *I do not roll my eyes or throw out my hip.*

Always Usually Sometimes Never

9 I focus on the needs of infants rather than my own feelings, thinking about how I would want to be treated if I were in a similar situation. I avoid thinking something like *This isn't the way I raised my kids.*

Always Usually Sometimes Never

10 I remain aware of the needs of the other children and the dynamics of the entire group while working one-on-one.

Always Usually Sometimes Never

Goals for More Positive and Frequent Interactions

Using the results of your assessment above, list three areas in which you need to improve. Here are some thoughts to consider: Do you go so slowly when working with one infant that you neglect the needs of the others? Do you typically try to do everything for infants instead of letting them help because it is easier, faster, and not as messy? Do you feel like your way of working with infants is the only way and that parents should just listen to you? Write three goals. Example: *I will talk to the infants more when I change them.*

1 ____________________

2 ____________________

3 ____________________

Basic Trust

The first year of life is when children need to acquire what psychologist Erik Erikson called "basic trust." Basic trust is the feeling an infant has of safety and security. Basic trust comes from responsive, predictable, nurturing care from familiar adults to whom the infant is attached. This is one of the reasons why consistency of infant teachers is so important at this age. A child's self-esteem and courage to explore, accept challenges, and move past mistakes or failures are founded on basic trust.

Can You Hold an Infant Too Much?

In many cultures, young infants are continually carried by their mothers, while in other areas of the world people believe babies should not be held "too much." And, of course, there's everything in between. People's beliefs and actions are based on cultural differences, parenting preferences, convenience, family influence, and teachers' beliefs. What's the right answer? In early childhood programs, teachers have the time and opportunity to hold infants often, and no research indicates that holding infants is detrimental to the child unless the practice prevents from developing gross-motor skills. There is evidence, however, that suggests that infants benefit from being held during periods of stress and times of play. My thought is that if babies aren't supposed to be held a lot, then they should be able to get from one place to another on their own. Some children like to be held a lot and others not so much. So respond to each infant accordingly.

Take Crying Seriously

Infants cry for many reasons, and it is never okay to ignore their cries. Take a look at the list of reasons why infants cry, and think about how you would respond personally to each of these situations. Are you the kind of person who can't wait to kick off your shoes after a full day of work? As adults, we are able to change our environment and comfort and help ourselves in most situations. Infants rely on adults to do these things for them. The infants in your care rely on you. Take their crying seriously—each child, every time, every cry.

Some Reasons Why Infants Cry

Infants have real and often painful or uncomfortable feelings that cause them to cry. Here are some of the reasons why they cry. Add two more of your ideas to the list.

- Hunger
- Tiredness
- Wet or soiled diapers
- Gas
- Teething
- Colic
- Clothing that is too tight or too warm
- Being too cold
- Being in an uncomfortable position
- Boredom
- Overstimulation
- Sudden changes, such as loud noises
- Bright lights
- Being picked up abruptly
- ______________________________
- ______________________________

9 Tips about Infants and Crying

1. Sometimes when infants' reasons for crying are not obvious, you will have to respond in a trial-and-error manner. This may even happen with babies you know well.
2. Often infants become impatient and easily upset by things during periods when they are attaining new skills, such as learning to walk. Their tolerance for frustration in other areas is limited while they focus their efforts on developing new competencies.
3. Infants may also become upset when something pleasurable stops, such as when you turn and give your attention to someone else or put away a toy.
4. Crying from infants sometimes indicates impatience because you are not meeting their needs fast enough. (I know you're moving as fast as you can, but think about how much you dislike waiting in line at a superstore.)
5. Observe infants who are frustrated and decide whether to assist immediately by helping them, making the situation easier to cope with, or letting them work things out. It's a difficult balance to know when to step in and when to hold off a bit when infants are upset.
6. You may not always be able to solve babies' concerns, such as a parent leaving or transitioning to a sleep time, but you can acknowledge their feelings and respond sympathetically.
7. Infants differ widely in their ability to quiet themselves when they are upset. That means your responses to comfort each baby will also differ widely. One child may just need your quick reassurance, while another may need to be held for a while when upset.
8. Infants are wired to do what they need to do to have their needs met. If you do not respond consistently to positive attempts from infants, such as smiling or holding out their arms, they may learn to rely primarily on crying as a means of getting your attention.
9. If you are working with infants who you are having trouble comforting, get the support of other teachers and staff. Infants' failure to respond to your attempts to console them is not an indication of your failure as a teacher. Rely on your entire team.

"That's not how we do it at home."

Acknowledging and Responding to Cultural Differences

As in almost everything, cultural practices in how families respond to crying and upset infants differ. Some families respond to crying quickly and consistently, while others respond only to sustained crying. Think about the following questions to better understand your own perspective and those of the families in your programs.

1 How were you comforted or helped as a child?

____

____

2 What is your personal view about responding to infants who are crying or upset?

____

____

3 What is the policy of your center or program about responding to infants who are crying and upset?

____

____

4 How can knowing the parents' practices at home help you better care for their infant in your program?

____

____

5 Give an example of how we tend to generalize about cultures.

____

____

6 If parents carry their child secured to their front or back at home, how is this information useful to providing more responsive care in your program?

____

____

7 If the parents want teachers to carry their child as they do at home, how can you accommodate this request?

____

____

Although you cannot always duplicate or accommodate what infants are familiar with and what families do at home, you should know as much as you can. Be sensitive and understand that it will be hard for some infants to adjust and to experience new situations. Many infants will need a great deal of holding and comforting.

What Infants Need from You

What infants need from you is a sense of familiarity, acceptance, and safety in their environment and relationships. How do you provide this? Try the following:

Communicate. Listen, smile, and talk with infants; babble when they babble.

Play. Retrieve toys and play peekaboo, hide-and-seek, and other games.

Care. Meet the physical needs of infants by feeding them, changing them, and helping them to sleep.

Soothe. Sing to babies and rock them when they are tired.

Hold. Cradle and hold infants when they feel small or sad or want to get or give attention and love.

Praise. Notice and communicate pleasure over newfound skills, such as creeping, climbing, holding, dropping, or adding new sounds and words.

Redirect. Change nonmobile infants' positions or locations in the room to help them discover new possibilities when they are bored.

Observe. Watch for the kinds of things that make infants happy and interested, such as toys, talk, and things to explore and play with.

Protect. Notice when infants need quiet and the chance to be alone.

Is It Possible to Work with Infants and Not Interact with Them?

It may seem to most of you that it is impossible to work with infants and not have positive and frequent interactions with them. Yet many infant teachers, in attempting to be efficient, tend to rush through care times like diapering and feeding to "get it done." So teachers who are caring for infants are not really interacting at all. Here's what I know from being an infant teacher: you can change all the diapers of the children and feel like you can check that off your list, but someone is going to wet or worse at some point. When you are caring for and educating infants, you can never complete your work, because it is ongoing and changing as they develop. In fact, I believe that many of you love the early childhood profession because it is so full of action and because every day brings different struggles and benefits. Does that sound like you?

Although interacting with infants includes communication, I am going to devote an entire chapter to the emerging language skills of infants because their language acquisition plays an important role in their later academic success, beginning with literacy skills. And you can play a huge role in helping infants develop language. The vocabulary of children of chatty moms is greater than that of children who have quieter parents or of those who do not speak directly to their children. Interesting, right? How infants communicate is next.

OPTIMIZE YOUR KNOWLEDGE

1 Name a time in the routine of infants that you or others may not consider as a **learning time.** What can infants learn during that period?

2 Observe a teacher in an infant room and describe her **positive interactions,** including physical gestures, nonverbal communication, and verbal reassurance or encouragement.

3 Explain how you could better accommodate the **cultural preferences** of a family in caring for their infant.

5 How Infants Communicate

5

Although infants may not talk, I realize that their communication is complex and intentional.

- Always
- Usually
- Sometimes
- Never

The Importance of Language

Language does more than simply represent our thoughts and feelings; it shapes and directs our thinking and emotions. A language-rich environment is important in encouraging cognitive development during the early years. Children are tuned in to language from birth. The first feeding begins the lifelong give-and-take of communication that culminates in dinner parties years later. The infant gurgles; the adult smiles and comments in response. The adult soothes; the infant sighs in response. From sighing, cooing, and babbling to first words, an infant learns that language is a powerful tool in human society.

Lots to Say without Any Words!

Although infants may not be able to talk right away, you will be amazed by the range of sounds they can make almost as soon as they are born. These varied sounds result from the infant's developing larynx or voice box. Actually, infants can make more sounds than we can as adults. If you really pay attention to the sounds each baby in your care makes and when, you'll start to understand that specific sounds indicate specific needs or wants. So remember: infants are saying a lot even though they may not have any distinguishable words until around twelve months of age.

What are some of the sounds infants in your care make, and what do you think they are trying to say? Note the sound or cry in the chart below by writing out phonetically how it sounds.

Sounds Infants Make

Sound Infant Uses to Communicate	What the Infant Is Saying

How Speech Typically Develops

Birth	3 Months	6 Months	9 Months	12 Months
Coo and gurgle	Make vowels sounds, *ah* and *ooh*	Babble, *bah-bah*	Imitate speech sounds	Say first spontaneous word, *mama, dada*

Physical Communication Comes before Verbal Communication

Babies can communicate physically before they communicate verbally. Newborns turn their heads to their mothers' bodies to find their breast. Babies turn their head away from a bottle or spoon when they aren't hungry anymore or don't like the taste. Infants point to things they want, wave, hug, and even make the gesture, "more," all before they can speak. Amazing! List some ways you've seen infants communicate physically. Can you name five ways?

1 ______________________________

2 ______________________________

3 ______________________________

4 ______________________________

5 ______________________________

Sign Language and Infants

Since infants communicate physically before verbally, it makes sense that they can easily learn sign language. Even if you don't know sign language, you could learn a few words. Research shows that children and infants who use sign language show stronger language development. Check out the following three signs and what they mean.

My Baby Had Something to Tell Me

I remember, as a parent, trying to feed one of my children a bottle, and she wouldn't take it. I knew she was hungry, but I couldn't figure out why she wouldn't take the bottle. I tried burping her, changing her diaper, and giving her that bottle again and again. She wasn't going to drink it. Finally, I unscrewed the bottle top, smelled the contents, and realized the expressed breast milk had spoiled. I prepared a new bottle, and she happily drank it all. Infants communicate in powerful ways. We just have to be willing to listen.

More Speech Developmental Milestones

7 days
Infants can distinguish their mother's voice from another woman's voice.

2 weeks
Infants can distinguish their father's voice from another man's voice.

3 months
Infants can make vowel sounds.

6 to 8 months
Infants have added a few consonant sounds to the vowel sounds and may say "dada" or "mama" but do not yet attach the sounds to individuals.

1 year
Infants will attach "mama" or "dada" to the right person.

1 year
Infants can respond to one-step commands. "Give it to me, please."

Communication Is Complex

What Is Speech?

Speech is the oral form of language. Language is a code made up of rules that include what words mean, how to make them, how to put them together, and what word combinations are best in what situations. Sounds complicated—and it is, if you think about learning a second language at your age. But for infants learning to speak their native language, it is a natural process that begins with imitation, trial and error, and lots of practice. I'm still learning new vocabulary words. How about you?

Understanding Words

Even before they can physically speak, children generally understand far more of what we say than they can articulate themselves.

Receptive language: what children understand when others speak to them

Expressive language: what children can say to others using words

Speech Development: Every Coo Counts

The first coo or babble of every infant brings an onslaught of adult celebration and excitement worthy of calling Grandma. The race is on for whether "mama" or "dada" will be a child's first word. Although speech development is a natural process, our verbal interactions with children help them learn to communicate.

15 Ways to Encourage an Infant's Language Development

1. Speak as you normally would. There is no need to oversimplify your own language or use baby talk, although infants do respond more to language that is higher in pitch or more exaggerated.
2. Put words to the child's actions. "Ethan is using his spoon."

3 Describe what you are doing. "Miss Chandra is washing Ethan's hands."

4 Use nouns more than pronouns. Call everyone by name, including yourself. "Miss Chandra is changing Ethan's diaper. That feels much drier, doesn't it, Ethan?"

5 Respond to crying and cooing. "Ethan, you must be hungry. Is that why you are crying?" "Ethan is talking to me. Miss Chandra likes the way Ethan talks."

6 Describe what the child is doing with lots of adjectives and adverbs. "Ethan, you are rolling the small ball quickly."

7 Listen and respond to a child's words and sounds, letting the give-and-take of conversation occur. After you say something, pause to give the child a chance to respond. "Would you like to roll the ball again, Ethan?"

8 Model language by using words and gestures. "Ethan, please come sit in the blue chair."

9 Expand a child's single-word utterances. "*Ba.*" "Ethan, you're right. That is a big green ball."

10 Name the child's possible feelings. "Ethan, you get angry when someone eats your food."

11 Allow for silent pauses and times. Talk to the child, but avoid bombarding her with language.

12 Ask the child questions even before you know he can verbally answer. "Do you see the bird sitting in that tree, Ethan?"

13 Encourage children to name objects by pointing to or retrieving items. "Ethan, will you hand Miss Chandra the book?" "Would Ethan like to point to the picture of the train?"

14 Let the child feel language. Place the child's hand on your neck while you talk, or let him feel the air coming from your mouth when you speak.

15 Construct and pose questions that require a child to answer with more than "yes" or "no." "Ethan, would you like a cup of water or a cup of milk?"

Reading Books and Singing Songs

Learning to speak is a natural process, but teachers who role-model appropriate conversation skills and use language frequently help children master language development more easily and expose children to more words, increasing their vocabulary. Infants learn language during the course of daily routines through rich conversation, singing, and reading. Read to infants. Even a newborn can benefit from the nurturing and language experience of being read to. Sing songs and make up silly songs. Here's some interesting information about infants and their response to singing. Infants can

- Recognize the familiar melodies of songs before they understand the meanings of words or what the song means.
- Imitate your language sounds in a kind of musical conversation with their own cooing and vocalizations. They wait for their turn and respond during pauses. (Have you ever experienced this with an infant?)
- Respond to singing and talking by waving their arms, kicking their feet, and smiling.
- Start moving to the beat as they are able to move.

So chat it up with the infants you care for by describing what you are doing and what they are doing, by asking questions, and by making meaning of the sounds and words they do make. Infants express themselves in many ways, and you can make sense of their communication and speech if you just pay attention. Next, you'll take a look at helping infants to settle and sleep and learn how to make sure sleeping times are safe.

OPTIMIZE YOUR KNOWLEDGE

1 Put the following **speech milestones** in order of typical development.

______ Says first word
______ Makes vowel sounds
______ Coos and gurgles
______ Babbles
______ Imitates speech sounds

2 How could you **encourage** an infant's language development in the following situations? Write what you would say.

▶ An infant, Simone, is picking up small pieces of cereal and feeding herself. What could you say? (*Hint:* Don't forget to use your name and the child's name instead of pronouns.)

____

____

____

▶ You are going to wash an infant's hands after diapering her. What could you say?

____

____

____

3 Observe an adult talking to an infant. Record the things the adult says or does and how that causes the baby to **pay attention and show responsiveness** by looking at the adult, smiling, or kicking his feet.

6 Helping Infants Settle and Sleep

6

I realize that helping infants learn to move from awake to asleep and back again is an important part of the curriculum for infants.

- Always
- Usually
- Sometimes
- Never

Rock-a-Bye-Baby Quiz

Let's start with a quiz about sleep. How much do you know about infants and sleep? The answers might surprise you. Answer the following statements by circling "True" or "False" based on typically developing babies.

1	true	false	As infants grow, the total hours of sleep they need decreases, but the length of sleep increases.
2	true	false	You should always put babies to sleep on their backs no matter how old they are.
3	true	false	During the first twelve months, most children have spent more time awake than asleep.
4	true	false	Most infants need complete quiet to sleep.

Ready for the Answers?

1 True. Newborns need as much as sixteen hours of sleep in a twenty-four-hour period, but they may only sleep for two hours at a time. Twelve-month-olds need about fourteen hours of sleep but may sleep as long as ten hours at night, if their parents are lucky!

2 True. Read statement 2 again, and always put infants to sleep on their backs. Children who are put to sleep on their backs are significantly less likely to develop sudden infant death syndrome (SIDS). Older infants may turn onto their stomachs to sleep, but as an early childhood professional, you must always put them down to sleep on their backs. Remember the phrase "Back to sleep, front to play." If you are putting infants on the floor for supervised playtime with you being right there, you may place them on their stomachs so they begin to develop upper body strength. If they become tired of trying to raise their heads or turn over, place them on their backs again. Small periods of supervised tummy time are good for infants.

3 False. During the first twelve months of life, most infants spend more time asleep than awake. By two years of age, children spend about 40 percent of their time asleep. Adequate sleep is essential for children's development, physically and mentally.

4 False. Fetuses actually begin to hear in the womb at about twenty-three weeks of age. Babies who were exposed in utero to noises such as blenders, vacuum cleaners, or barking dogs are usually not scared of these sounds. In fact, those babies can sleep comfortably with noise and may not even awaken to a barking dog or the making of a smoothie. Although a calm environment can be more conducive to sleep, most infants easily adjust to sleeping in a room where other children are chatting or even crying. Infants are often more adaptable than you realize.

Back to sleep, front to play

Always put infants down to sleep on their backs. They may choose to turn over to their stomachs if they are developmentally able, but always place them to sleep on their backs.

Lots of Sleep for Infants

As with every area of development and growth, the amount of sleep infants need varies with their temperament and age. As you learned from the infant sleep quiz, newborns do sleep a great deal of time in short segments. As babies grow, the total amount of sleep they need gradually decreases and the length of their nighttime sleep increases. Check out the chart that follows for very general guidelines of the amount of sleep infants need based on their age. Remember, every baby is different.

Sleep Tight Chart

Age	Total Sleep Hours	Total Hours of Nighttime Sleep	Total Hours of Daytime Sleep
Newborn	16	8-9	8
1 month	15.5	8-9	7
3 months	15	9-10	4-5
6 months	14	10	4
9 months	14	11	3
1 year	14	11	3

Take a look at the chart above. As the number of hours children sleep at night increases, what happens to the number of hours they sleep during the day? Circle the answer:

The number of hours they sleep during the day

decreases increases

You'll also notice that young infants usually sleep a lot in your program, so learning to determine how infants demonstrate that they are sleepy and knowing how to soothe each infant to sleep is critical to good care. Helping young infants get enough sleep is a large portion of your curriculum.

Naps and Infants

By six weeks of age, many babies begin to develop more regular sleep patterns, and their confusion of night and day ends. As they age, helping them establish healthy sleep patterns is one of your primary goals. From two months to six months, infants usually have three naps a day; that changes to two naps after six months. Children under six months of age typically have midmorning, afternoon, and late-afternoon naps. The duration of these naps varies for each child but is usually around two hours.

While helping infants develop a sleep pattern is important, remember that this pattern evolves as they grow. Your responsibility as an early childhood professional is to understand when infants are sleepy and let them sleep. It is never okay to keep infants from sleeping or to wake them up intentionally. Sleep, whether nighttime or daytime naps, is a physiological necessity for proper development. Don't ever try to keep a baby from sleeping.

SIDS Is Serious

SIDS Is Sudden Infant Death Syndrome

- Researchers and medical professionals do not know what causes SIDS.
- SIDS is the leading cause of death of children aged one to twelve months.
- One out of five SIDS cases occurs when a child is with someone other than the parent.
- Infants who are placed on their stomachs to sleep are eighteen times more likely to die from SIDS.
- Follow safe sleep policies to reduce the risk of SIDS.
- *Don't* put in a crib:
  - Bottles
  - Blankets
  - Stuffed animals
  - Loose bedding
  - Bumper pads
  - Toys
  - Pillows
  - Sleeping wedges
- *Do* put in a crib:
  - Firm crib mattress
  - Fitted, crib-sized sheet on mattress
  - An infant, on back, in sleepwear

The Dos and Don'ts of Safe Sleep for Infants Twelve Months and Younger

- Don't put infants to sleep on a chair, sofa, cushion, beanbag chair, waterbed, or adult bed.
- Do place infants on their backs on a firm mattress, with a fitted sheet, in a crib approved by the Consumer Product Safety Commission. For the latest update on safety standards, check out www.cpsc.gov.
- Don't put anything in the crib but the infant. No bottles, blankets, stuffed animals, loose bedding, bumper pads, toys, pillows, or sleeping wedges.
- Do place the child in appropriate sleepwear as an alternative to using blankets. Appropriate sleep clothing includes sleepers, wearable blankets, and sleep sacks.
- Don't put more than one infant in a crib for sleeping—not even siblings or multiples.
- Do keep the temperature in the sleep area comfortable for a lightly clothed adult.
- Don't let babies get too hot. They may be too hot if they are sweating, breathing heavily, have flushed cheeks, damp hair, or a heat rash.
- Do educate families about these safe sleep practices and encourage them to implement the practices at home.
- Don't allow anyone to smoke in the infant sleep area in a child care center, family child care provider's home, or the infant's home.
- Don't allow a family to request their infant sleep in any way other than on their backs without a note from the child's pediatrician noting the position in which the infant should sleep, the medical reason why, and for what length of time.
- Do realize that safe sleep habits reduce the risk of SIDS.

winning ways

Suggest that parents share a room with their infants twelve months and under, but not their bed. Room sharing, not bed sharing, reduces SIDS (sudden infant death syndrome) by up to 50 percent. Parents can place the infant's crib in their bedroom or sleep area.

10 Ways Babies Tell You When They Are Sleepy

Infants may not be able to talk, but most little ones do give many cues and signs when they are sleepy. A good early childhood professional observes all babies closely to notice and learn their individual sleep cues. Young children can go from sleepy to overtired very quickly. Respond to these cues to guide infants to good sleep habits and longer, more restful sleep. Here are some signs and cues to look for:

1. Rubbing eyes
2. Pausing or decreasing activity
3. Wriggling back and forth uncomfortably
4. Fussing, being cranky or irritable
5. Pulling on ears, hair, or clothing
6. Looking away or staring off
7. Becoming uninterested in surroundings
8. Yawning
9. Turning head from side to side
10. Crying

Helping Infants to Fall Asleep

Once you recognize sleep readiness signs, you can help babies to learn to calm themselves, establish healthy sleep patterns, and fall asleep more easily. Remember, this is your curriculum: responding to the individual needs of each baby. Some infants fall asleep if you place them in the crib when they are tired, and others need you to rock or hold them. Here are some tips for helping little ones drift off more easily:

- Rock the baby.
- Give the infant a bottle.
- Walk around with the child.
- Gently bounce the infant.
- Sing to the baby.
- Carry the baby in baby carrier on your body.
- Allow the child to have a pacifier.
- Dress the infant in comfortable, warm sleepwear.

Crying It out—Good or Bad?

Is it appropriate for early childhood professionals to put infants in their cribs and let them cry until they fall asleep? This question is a hot topic for educators and parents. Peoples' thoughts about letting children cry themselves to sleep are based on personal preference, cultural norms, adult convenience, and how they were parented. While there are a few infants who do not respond well to adult soothing and may need to cry a few minutes to fall asleep, the majority of young children can benefit from having adults help them make the transition from wakefulness to sleep. Putting infants in their cribs when they are drowsy but not completely asleep does help them learn to self-soothe or put themselves to sleep. But crying for more than a few minutes does not help, since infants do not usually develop a regular sleep cycle until they're about six months.

As the mother of four, an early childhood expert, and advocate of the American Academy of Pediatrics' recommendations, I believe that "crying it out" is not the best option for infants. Why? The soothing process helps infants understand that the sleep state is a comfortable place to enter and a secure place to remain. The bond formed during rocking and snuggling builds adult-infant trust and makes the world more predictable. And isn't that what your job is? You help young children grow and learn in an environment that is healthy and loving. You rock and snuggle and sing and comfort. They are infants, and they will only be infants for one year.

What to Do If Infants Fall Asleep and They Are Not in Their Cribs

Many devices transport, protect, or secure infants: car seats, strollers, high chairs, swings, and bouncy seats. In a car, the best and only option is having the infant in an approved Consumer Products Safety Commission car seat. Children often fall asleep in car seats and other devices, but the safest place for them to sleep is in their crib. If they fall asleep in a swing or stroller, carefully transfer them to their crib. Likewise, if they arrive in car seats asleep, move them to their cribs. Even though they may look comfortable or you may run the risk of waking them, car seats are for protection in cars and not for sleeping unless cars are in motion. Children's position in car seats can reduce their respiratory capacity, and unsupervised sleeping in car seats is associated with SIDS. Infants should always sleep on their backs in cribs.

The Importance of an Individualized Sleep Plan

Infants should always be allowed to sleep when they are sleepy. Trying to keep babies awake is unacceptable and unhealthy for them. The primary activity of the brain during early development is sleeping. Although allowing for individual sleeping patterns in a group care setting means some children are asleep while others are playing and making noise, most children get used to sleeping with noise around them.

The sleep amounts, patterns, and preferences of infants change dramatically in the first year. Knowing that sleep is a biological necessity, you should observe each infant in your care closely and respond to individual cues, helping each baby establish a somewhat predictable, yet evolving, sleep pattern. Helping children move from awake to sleep and sleep to awake will consume much of your time. With lots of sleeping comes lots of energy for learning. Ready to discover about how infants learn?

OPTIMIZE YOUR KNOWLEDGE

1 How much **daytime sleep** does a typical six-month-old need? Refer to the chart on page 56. __________

2 List three ways to help **reduce SIDS.**

1 ______________________________

2 ______________________________

3 ______________________________

3 Observe an early childhood professional putting an infant to sleep. Write a few sentences about what you see. Note the ways the educator helps **soothe the baby.**

____

____

____

____

7 How Infants Learn

7

I help infants learn by offering them many opportunities to explore and responding to their interests and curiosities.

- Always
- Usually
- Sometimes
- Never

Learning and Teaching

Infants are learning all the time, including during routines and transitions. Direct instruction—what most people view as teaching—rarely plays any part in very young children's experiences, yet adults are constantly concerned with education, even that of infants. Why the concern over teaching? Because parents want children to learn and because teachers like to teach. Everyone is interested in what is best for the children, and that means helping infants learn. Often, however, adults think that learning can only happen when teachers instruct. When educators respond to infants' drive to learn, that's teaching! And what infants are interested in learning is most often expressed through play.

Assisted Discovery

According to the psychologist Lev Vygotsky, the role of education is to provide experiences that are challenging for each child and achievable with sensitive adult guidance. The Vygotsky approach to learning is one of assisted discovery, in which teachers

- Create an exciting environment
- Encourage children's natural curiosity
- Engage in lots of dialogue with children
- Ask children questions

When Do You Start Teaching Children to Read?

My Story about Infants and Academics

At one time in my career as an early childhood professional, I was the director of a large employer-sponsored child development center. Many of the parents were interested in the educational aspects of the program, as any parent should be.

During a tour of the facility, a new mother who was exploring care options for her infant asked, "When do you teach the children to learn to read?" I started to respond with my usual talk about literacy and how children learn to read, but for some reason, I blurted out, "At six weeks." "You start teaching the children to read when they are six weeks old?" the somewhat surprised yet impressed mother questioned. "Yes, we have an extensive early literacy program that begins at six weeks, when the children enter the center. We integrate the child into a language-rich environment in which teachers are trained to purposefully engage with each child through conversations, reading, singing, and fingerplays."

Hey, it's the truth. Isn't that what good infant programs do? Early childhood professionals are teaching young children—even infants—to learn to read through their positive interactions. The mom quickly signed up her newborn for enrollment.

We Want Real Learning, Not Just Play

Many families, even those of infants, worry that their children will not get the education they need. In addition, many parents pay a great deal of money for their program and often comment, "All this play is really costly. I want my child to learn, not just play." Sound familiar? Parents and even some teachers don't always have an appropriate perspective on how infants learn. Infants, and all children, learn best through active, hands-on play. So your role is twofold: (1) structuring and organizing your environment to best promote play and (2) responding to and initiating ideas to enhance play. Do you maximize learning through play? Take the following self-assessment.

Do You Maximize Learning Experiences for Infants?

1 ☐ yes ☐ no I respond appropriately to infants' play initiatives, such as smiling at me, offering me a toy, or holding up arms to me.

2 ☐ yes ☐ no I avoid overwhelming infants with my own activities, such as ulling them up repeatedly when they are not interested or forcing them to scribble when they are reluctant.

3 ☐ yes ☐ no I adapt my interactions based on infants' cues, such as finding something appropriate to mouth if they want to put things in their mouths or giving infants something soft to throw if they want to throw.

4 ☐ yes ☐ no I change an activity based on their interest like letting older infants play with the glue instead of gluing items.

5 ☐ yes ☐ no I communicate with infants in a variety of ways, responding with a reassuring word, sign language gesture, facial expression, or touch.

6 ☐ yes ☐ no I recognize the individual style of children's play: the child who quickly becomes involved, the one who is hesitant and needs encouragement, and the child who is excited and needs guidance to focus on one play activity.

7 ☐ yes ☐ no I help infants master new challenges by waiting to see if they can figure out the challenge by themselves, intervening before they get frustrated, and demonstrating a solution if they are about to give up.

8 ☐ yes ☐ no I allow infants to explore materials by letting them discover different uses and possibilities that I may not have intended; I do not show them the "right way" to use the material.

9 ☐ yes ☐ no I encourage infants to persist, work hard, and achieve goals, but I understand that the process is just as important as or even more important than the outcome.

10 ☐ yes ☐ no I encourage infants in their explorations.

11 ☐ yes ☐ no I help infants enjoy playing and interacting with other children by setting up an appropriate environment, providing duplicates of toys and materials, and modeling and guiding appropriate ways to interact.

12 ☐ yes ☐ no I keep infants safe but allow them reasonable risks while they explore.

Read to Infants

Just as they develop language skills long before being able to speak, infants also develop literacy skills long before being able to read. What you do, or don't do, has a lasting impact on their reading skills and literacy competency, not just as infants but for years to come. Does this mean that if you don't help infants with early literacy, they won't become good readers? No, there's always hope that every child will succeed, but reading aloud to young children is so critical that the American Academy of Pediatrics recommends that doctors prescribe reading to infants and tell parents at regular checkups about the importance of reading: "Children develop much of their capacity for learning in the first three years of life, when their brains grow to 90 percent of their eventual adult weight." As described in chapter 2, "Infants Are Amazing," when you talk, sing, and read to infants, links among their brain cells are strengthened and new cells and links are formed. According to America Reads, "Despite the considerable evidence of a relationship between reading regularly to a child and that child's later reading development, six in ten babies and five in ten toddlers are not read to regularly by parents or family members." You must read to infants regularly and inform parents about the importance of reading to their babies.

The Value of Play

Infants learn or acquire new skills and understandings about the world and themselves through play, exploration, and living each new day. Good caregivers value and encourage play as natural, integral parts of infants' experiences in child care. You need to be aware of their emerging skills and probable next developmental steps to plan the learning environment and guide interactions.

7 Tips for Supporting Infants' Play

1. Play should be driven by the infants' interests and timetable, not the adult's.
2. Play is something that is done with infants, not to them.
3. Play with infants only after you observe them and decide if you have an opportunity simply to watch or a moment to engage or play with them.
4. Play with infants initially by imitating their play.
5. Play with infants by demonstrating a similar activity that continues their flow of interest.
6. Play is enhanced when you recognize infants' efforts by describing their activities and/or asking questions about them.
7. Play should be praised by acknowledging infants for their successes and efforts during play.

A Message from the Book *Prime Times*

Initiating or Responding? Actually Both.

Responding to children's needs and interests is considered a keystone of good care and education. But this does not mean that teachers just sit back and respond—that they never try something completely new, that they never start something, that everything they do has to follow in a very literal way from something they have noticed through observation. How boring that would be for both children and teachers alike! Clever, creative, sensitive teachers experiment all the time—*Let's try this; Let's change that; I have an idea; I wonder what would happen if . . .*

The key is that when something new is offered or is placed in the environment, excellent teachers pay close attention to how children respond. Excellent care and education involve responding, initiating, and always paying close attention to what children are doing and saying.

Through the Eyes of an Infant

What does good care and education look like to infants? If they could ask questions about their own care and education, they might ask the following.

Will you hold me? Will you hold me when I want to be held or need to be held, even if it's a lot?

Will you talk to me? When I babble or coo, will you listen and talk back? When you talk to me, will you look at me and have real conversations?

Will you read to me? Will you read to me even if I am only six weeks old?

Will you give me places to move? Pull myself up? Reach? Kick? Jump? Climb up? Climb in? Climb over? Climb on? Go through? Go under? Go in and out? See myself?

Will you let me out if I want? If you put me in an infant swing or bouncy chair, can I get out when I want to get out? Can I get out of my crib when I can't sleep? How often do I get out of the room? Do I go outside every day? Do I get out of the stroller or cart to walk or crawl around?

Will you let me play? Will you let me play with messy things like water, sand, dough, and paint? Are there real-life objects and toys that I can reach and touch? Transport? Push/pull? Collect/dump? Throw?

Will you let me do it myself? Do I get to try to feed myself as soon as I can hold a spoon, bottle, or cup? Will you ask me to help you even if that means it takes you longer?

Will you appreciate me? Will you like me as a person? Will you make me feel good about being me? Will you like me if I am different from you?

Infants learn and acquire new skills and understandings through play, exploration, and living each and every day. Infant teachers need to value and encourage play as a natural, integral part of children's experiences in your program. Be aware of infants' emerging skills and probable next developmental steps so you can plan the learning environment accordingly. Now let's focus on guiding infants' behavior. Socialization and guidance are not discipline—they help children learn how to act in socially acceptable ways.

OPTIMIZE YOUR KNOWLEDGE

1 In your own words, explain the difference between **teaching and learning**.

____

____

____

____

2 Pretend you are taking an infant's parent on a tour of your program. How would you explain the **importance of play**? Write what you would say.

____

____

____

____

3 List three questions you could ask infants who are holding toys that would **support and enhance** their play.

1 ______________________________

2 ______________________________

3 ______________________________

8 Guiding Infants' Behavior

8

I understand that discipline is not about punishment but about guiding infants to make safe choices and act in socially acceptable ways.

- Always
- Usually
- Sometimes
- Never

Discipline for Infants: Really?

The thought of disciplining infants may seem ridiculous or even wrong. Yet every time babies reach up to tug your hair and you gently loosen their clasp, or when they pull an unsafe object to their mouth and you redirect their attention while easing the object from their grasp, you are guiding the infants' behavior. You are intervening, setting limits, redirecting, and, yes, disciplining them. Discipline is about teaching infants to make safe choices and to act in socially acceptable ways. It's about acknowledging their emotions and helping them control their reactions, about understanding how the world works and their place in it. By guiding infants' behavior in a positive way and thinking about discipline as a teachable moment, not a punishable one, you can help the infants in your program learn and succeed.

It's a Baby's Job to Test the Limits

Since young children's job is to try to learn to behave in the world while trying to make sense of it at the same time, they will test the limits of their environment and experience the consequences of their behavior. Exploring and testing are tremendous challenges for infants and their teachers. The unsafe and often frustrating behavior of infants is usually repetitive and sometimes annoying. You might think, "Don't they know they will fall if they pull up on that chair?" Most times, no. Infants don't yet understand the laws of balance and physics. They learn by exploring and experimenting, and it's your responsibility to keep them safe from harm, make them feel secure, and guide them to socially acceptable behaviors. A big job? You bet. And the most important one of all.

Guiding Infants' Behavior

Although guiding infants' behavior starts on day one, it certainly doesn't happen in a day. Your goal as a teacher is to lovingly help babies start learning how to get along with others. Remember that socialization and guidance is a long journey that requires lots of patience and reminding on your part, but it's well worth the effort for the children and you.

I think you'll agree that guiding infants' behavior is one of the more complex and difficult tasks you face as an educator. Take a look at some of the first steps to help them as described in the assessment below. As you can tell from this book, I'm big on assessments because I believe they give you the opportunity to really evaluate your behavior and interactions with children in an honest and productive way. You can't know how to enhance your behavioral guidance if you don't know how you are really guiding. Read each statement and circle the answer that most closely describes your actions.

First Steps in Infant Socialization and Guidance: "How Do I Rate?"

Name: ______________________

Date: ______________________

Program: ______________________

Room: ______________________

1 I spend time with the infants in my care, playing, snuggling, and getting to know one another.

Always Usually Sometimes Never

2 I respond to each infant's needs by establishing a flexible general routine based on the child's cues.

Always Usually Sometimes Never

3 I create an environment with safe objects and areas that infants can explore, not one that requires me to say no often.

Always Usually Sometimes Never

4 I anticipate and prevent dangerous situations.

Always Usually Sometimes Never

5 I ignore infants' behavior that may be annoying but is appropriate and not harmful, such as constant babbling or dumping toys.

Always Usually Sometimes Never

6 I distract or redirect infants from things they shouldn't do—for example, by giving them a ball if they want to throw things.

Always Usually Sometimes Never

7 I give the infants lots of attention and encourage positive behavior.

Always Usually Sometimes Never

8 I give the infants the freedom to explore within limits.

Always Usually Sometimes Never

How Did You Rate?

So how did you rate? What did you notice about the majority of the assessment statements? The key to guiding infants is

1. Establishing a positive relationship with the infants in your care
2. Having an individual yet flexible routine for each infant
3. Creating a safe environment with lots of things and spaces that they can freely touch and explore
4. Ignoring developmentally appropriate behavior, such as dropping things or constant babbling
5. Redirecting infants to acceptable actions
6. Giving infants lots of positive attention

First Steps in Infant Socialization and Guidance

Newborns communicate by crying. That's how they tell adults that they're hungry or wet or don't feel well. Or maybe they're just seeking the attention and touch of a loving person. Each time you respond to infants' cries, you are reinforcing their behavior and helping them learn to communicate. In a sense, you're disciplining them. For infants, socialization and guidance involve consistently and responsively meeting their needs. This helps create a strong attachment between them and you. This positive teacher-child relationship provides the basic trust they need to help them comply when you tell them they shouldn't do something. It also encourages their desire to please you. Check chapter 3, "Individualized Care for Infants," for more information on basic trust.

Create the Right Routine and Environment for Each Infant

Provide generally structured daily routines but also learn to recognize and respond flexibly to infants' individual needs. As they become more mobile and initiate more contact with the environment, you will need to impose more limitations and structure to create safe spaces for them to explore and play.

Nurture each infant. **Children grow and learn best in an environment in which they feel comfortable and secure. Spend time playing and reading.**

Create an Environment of Yes, Not No

If infants constantly pull over a plant, remove the plant or any other unsafe object. Infants have plenty of opportunities to learn the word *no*. Create a "Yes" environment. Here's how:

Anticipate and prevent dangerous situations. Move breakable objects to higher shelves and put gates near stairs. Create a safe and healthy environment.

Ignore annoying behavior. Sometimes infants' actions can be annoying but not harmful. If they pull everything off the toy shelf, just take a deep breath. That's what infants do.

Distract or redirect each infant's behavior. Try to distract or redirect infants from things you don't want them to have or do. If they grab the spoon you are using to feed them, don't just take the spoons away; instead, give them their own spoon or interest them in some other toy or activity once the feeding is over. They'll then let go of the spoon you are using. It's easier to redirect infants to another interest than to simply take something away.

Acknowledge appropriate behavior. Infants seek approval and attention. Reward their appropriate behavior with words of praise and lots of hugs. Your positive attention is infants' most important reinforcement. Use it to encourage positive behavior.

Give each infant the freedom to explore within limits. Babies need freedom to explore but also limits. You need good judgment to provide both. Babies kept in bouncy seats or high chairs for much of the day have too little freedom and are too limited. They need freedom—a safe environment on the floor to explore and play.

7 Steps to Successfully Guiding Inappropriate Behavior

When older infants are hurting another child, damaging the physical environment, or about to hurt themselves, take these seven steps:

1. **Tell the child in a firm voice to stop.** Tell the child to stop in a firm but friendly voice. Speak at close range whenever possible, not from across the room. An adult's tone of voice can communicate approval or disapproval effectively before a baby can actually understand the words.
2. **Help the child stop the inappropriate behavior.** Redirect the child to a new activity or physically remove the child, the object, or the victim if necessary. Words often are not enough. Even when children understand the directive to stop, they may not have the willpower to stop. Giving a number of verbal warnings is not helpful. In fact, doing so can provide children with an incentive to continue doing what they are doing.
3. **Give a brief explanation of why the behavior is unacceptable.** Give brief, simple reasons why the behavior is unacceptable, keeping in mind the limits of young children's understanding of their own behavior. Explaining will help you stay calm, and it will help build their understanding so they can gradually make those judgments themselves and guide their own behavior. Reasons may be obvious to us but not to children.

4 **Tell the child the appropriate behavior and model it.** State and model the acceptable behavior. Say, "Be gentle with John," while stroking John's arm. Find an acceptable alternative when appropriate. If you are stopping children from doing something, don't just tell them what they cannot do—tell them what they can do as well.

5 **Offer the child choices.** Offer children reasonable choices whenever you can. Examples: "Do you want to finish your drink or get down and play?" Avoid implying a choice when there is none. "Would you like to give Joey a turn on the swing now?" is not appropriate unless a resounding "No!" from the happily swinging toddler is acceptable. When there is no choice, be prepared to help the child go along with the decision you have made.

6 **Validate the child's emotions.** Always recognize and acknowledge a child's feelings of anger, confusion, or hurt as legitimate. "I know that makes you angry when Tommy takes your toy, but you can't hit him. Tell him no." Or "It's frustrating when you can't get the toy to work the way you want it to. May I help you?"

7 **Recognize your own inability to deal with a particular situation.** Seek help if you are about to lose control or are too angry to handle the situation.

The Don'ts of Good Discipline

Don't shame or humiliate the child. Even saying, "You wet your pants again," can be a form of humiliation and shame. Instead, say, "Let's get you into some clean clothes."

Don't shake, jerk, squeeze, or physically indicate your disapproval. Working with infants is a challenging job, physically and mentally, but it is never okay to physically indicate your disapproval.

Don't call children names such as "bad," "ornery," "a handful." Saying a child is a "bad girl or boy" or otherwise implying that the child is the problem, instead of the behavior, is unacceptable.

Don't moralize or let too much of your anger come through. You may feel angry, and it's okay to tell a child you are angry, but you should never react in anger to an infant, as this will make an infant fearful and anxious. "It makes me angry when you hit me. Please touch me gently, like this."

Don't use "No" too often. Instead, use the positive "Hold on to the cup" and other words like "Stop" or "Please don't."

A Note about Temper Tantrums for Older Infants

What causes temper tantrums? Ever try to work some new sort of electronic gadget, only to find yourself tossing the manual, stomping your feet, and contemplating hurling the gizmo out the window? That's the adult version of a tantrum. Most of the time, a child who has a tantrum is also struggling with frustration. Frustration in children may be caused by

- Hunger
- Exhaustion
- Inability to communicate a need or desire
- Inability to produce a particular outcome—for example, work a toy
- Overstimulation, having too many things happening at once

Watching an infant have a tantrum can be frightening to parents, teachers, other children, and even the infant who is having the tantrum. Temper tantrums, like crying, are real expressions of distress, not usually something infants put on deliberately. Most infants in the throes of a temper tantrum need help to get out of it. The kind of help varies with the child. Some infants need to be held to get back in control. But for others, being held feels like restraint and only fuels the tantrum. Tantrums can be physically and emotionally exhausting for children. You can try to help infants avoid tantrums by

- Validating their frustration or concerns
- Helping them communicate by giving them words
- Allowing them to make their own personal choices when possible
- Helping them solve problems

Fortunately, temper tantrums don't last forever, although it may not feel that way. They're usually not cause for developmental concern, and they lessen in frequency and severity as children get older and learn to control and better express their emotions. As children better grasp their needs and wants, their levels of frustration decrease. Less frustration and more control mean fewer tantrums, and that makes everyone happier. Ever feel like throwing yourself on the floor of a grocery store kicking and screaming? Maybe it's just me.

A Note about Infants Biting

In even the best programs, periodic outbreaks of biting occur among infants, toddlers, and sometimes even preschoolers. This is an unavoidable consequence of young children in group care. When it happens, it's pretty scary, very frustrating, and very stressful for children, parents, and teachers. However unfortunate, biting is a natural phenomenon, not something to blame on anyone. No quick and easy solutions exist.

Why Do Children Bite?

Children bite for a variety of reasons. Sometimes it's for the simple oral sensory exploration of things. They put almost everything in their mouths, so why not other people? Biting happens when they feel crowded, want to be noticed, or want to obtain something, such as a toy. The lack of communication skills can also cause young ones to bite. For some, biting becomes a learned behavior, and they realize that biting does, in fact, get them what they want. Here are the steps to follow when an infant bites another child:

1. **Treat biting seriously.** Although biting is a developmentally appropriate behavior for infants, it is still inappropriate.
2. **Focus your attention on the bitten child.** Children who bite may be seeking your attention, even if it is negative attention. First, focus your attention on the child who has been bitten. Comfort the bitten infant.
3. **Remove the biter from the situation.** Respond to the child who bites in a cool, firm, and disapproving way. In a serious voice, tell the child, "No biting. Biting hurts."
4. **Provide appropriate ways to express frustration.** Talk to the child who bites in understandable terms. "I know you wanted the toy, but you can't bite. Next time use your words. Say 'I want the truck'" (even though an infants' words are just developing).
5. **Give the child positive reinforcement for not biting.** Make sure you give as much attention to an infant's appropriate behavior as to her inappropriate behavior. "I know you were really angry. Thank you for using your words."
6. **Give the child something acceptable to bite.** Give the infant something to bite—for example, a washcloth.

7 **Give the child attention when he behaves appropriately.** Children who bite repeatedly need love and attention when they are being good so they can learn that they can and will be noticed without doing something wrong. "Look how nicely you are playing with your friends. May I join you? It's fun to be around people who are kind."

Guiding infants to socially acceptable behavior starts when they are born, but your expectations should always be appropriate. Remember, you are working with infants. Help them succeed by creating a safe environment full of things to explore.

OPTIMIZING YOUR KNOWLEDGE

1 Explain why it is important to **guide the behavior** of young children, even infants.

____

____

____

____

2 What are some of the reasons that young infants have **temper tantrums**?

____

____

____

____

3 One infant bites another because the second one has claimed a toy. How would you **handle** the situation with each child?

____

____

____

____

For All You Do

Infants are amazingly complex individuals, and understanding them is no easy job. I hope this book, *Understanding Infants*, gave you greater insight into their growth and development and how they learn and communicate. A deeper knowledge of who infants are and how they interact with the world can help you develop more positive interactions and appropriate environments. Think about the amount of learning that takes place in that short year of infancy. You can play a powerful role in providing infants with the security, comfort, and stability they need to explore the world with confidence and trust in the adults around them. Here's to all the infant teachers. That's you, you NDS!

Certificate of Achievement

This certificate is presented to

____

for completing the professional development program:

Winning Ways for Early Childhood Professionals: Understanding Infants

__________ In-service hours

Redleaf Press®
www.redleafpress.org
800-423-8309

Gigi Schweikert
www.gigischweikert.com

The author and Redleaf Press have not verified the actual completion of the program by this participant.